Our Many Foods

Ellen Lawrence

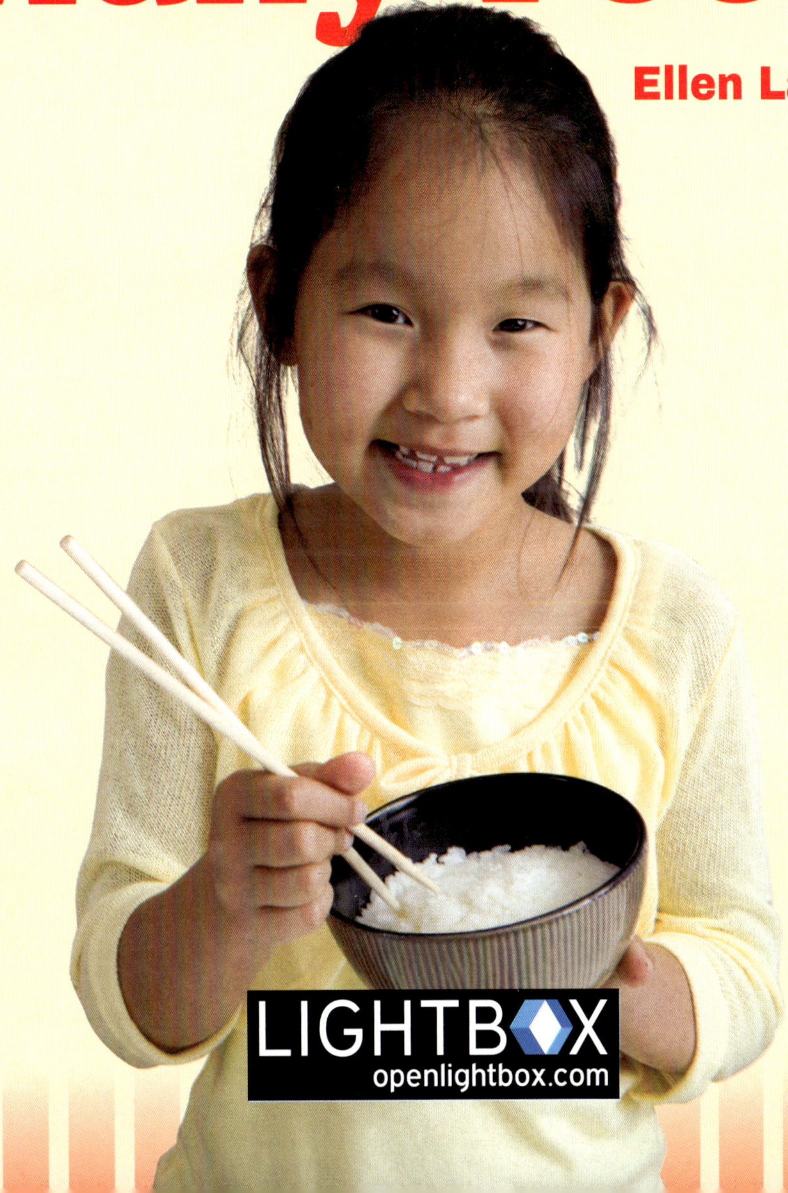

LIGHTBOX
openlightbox.com

Go to
www.openlightbox.com
and enter this book's
unique code.

ACCESS CODE

LBA97545

Lightbox is an all-inclusive digital solution for the teaching and learning of curriculum topics in an original, groundbreaking way. Lightbox is based on National Curriculum Standards.

OPTIMIZED FOR

- ✓ **TABLETS**
- ✓ **WHITEBOARDS**
- ✓ **COMPUTERS**
- ✓ **AND MUCH MORE!**

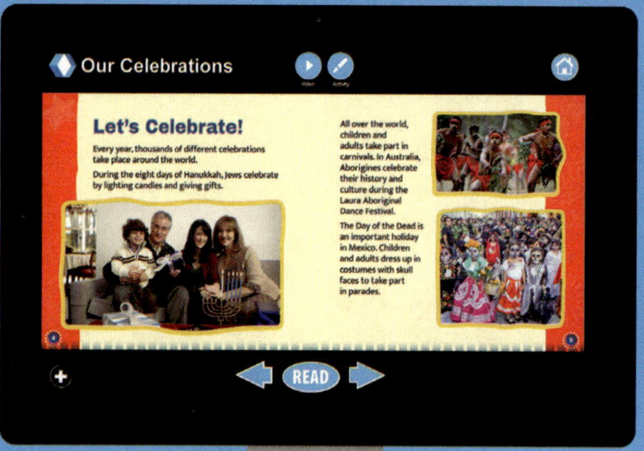

Copyright © 2019 Smartbook Media Inc. All rights reserved.

STANDARD FEATURES OF LIGHTBOX

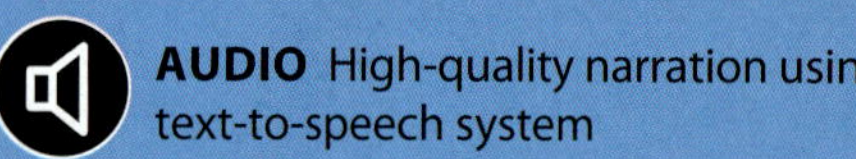

AUDIO High-quality narration using text-to-speech system

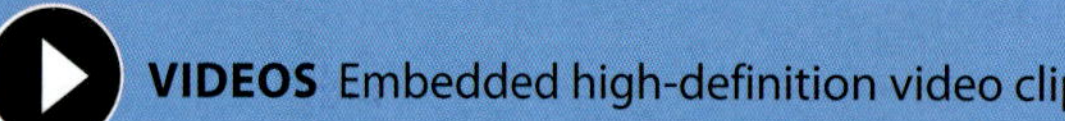

VIDEOS Embedded high-definition video clips

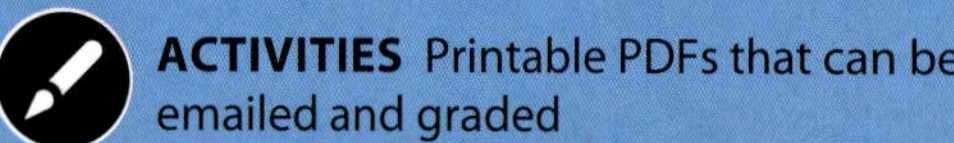

ACTIVITIES Printable PDFs that can be emailed and graded

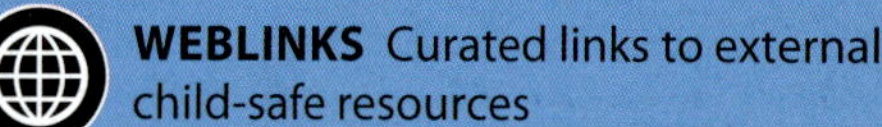

WEBLINKS Curated links to external, child-safe resources

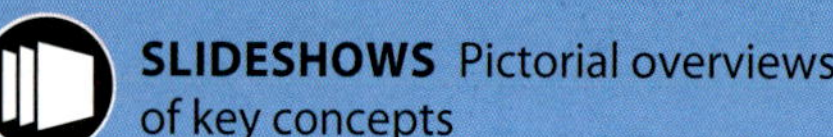

SLIDESHOWS Pictorial overviews of key concepts

INTERACTIVE MAPS Interactive maps and aerial satellite imagery

QUIZZES Ten multiple choice questions that are automatically graded and emailed for teacher assessment

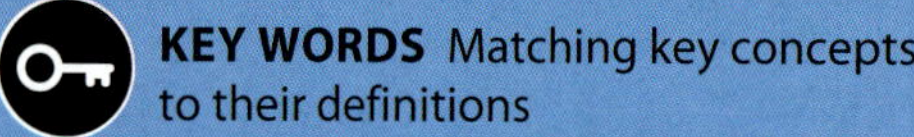

KEY WORDS Matching key concepts to their definitions

VIDEOS

WEBLINKS

SLIDESHOWS

QUIZZES

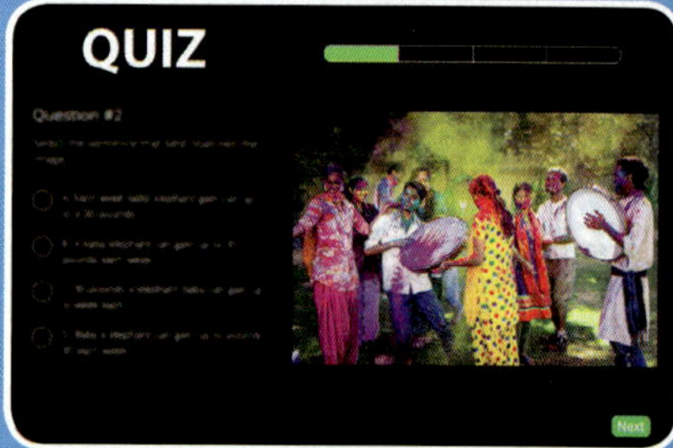

About Our World

Our Many Foods

What Foods Do We Eat?

It's porridge for breakfast in Namibia.

A lunch of sausage and fries in Germany.

A delicious dinner of vegetables and noodles in the United States.

Fruit is a popular food all over the world. In Malaysia, many people eat durian fruit. The flesh of this fruit smells like strong cheese and onions, but it tastes like custard. In Mexico, people eat black sapote fruit. Its nickname, the chocolate pudding fruit, says how it tastes!

A Very Important Food

There is one food that people eat all over the world—rice.

Rice is a type of grass plant. The rice grains we eat are the plant's seeds. People grow and eat more than 40,000 different types of rice!

Rice plants grow best in places where the land is very wet. Often farmers flood their rice fields with water from nearby rivers. In some places, farmers use water buffaloes to plow the wet, muddy fields before the rice is planted.

Almost half the rice grown in the United States comes from eastern Arkansas.

Delicious Bento Boxes

Imagine opening your lunchbox to see your favorite animal or cartoon character. In Japan, that's just what many children get to do every day.

The colorful lunchboxes are called bento boxes.

Japanese parents turn food into animal faces, superheroes, cars, flowers, and many other shapes.

The main food in a bento box is usually rice balls. The meal might also include seaweed, mini hot dogs, salmon, eggs, cubes of cheese, pickled vegetables, and fruit.

Sweets for Diwali

The festival of Diwali is celebrated by Hindu, Sikh, and Jain people around the world. Diwali is also known as the festival of lights.

Diwali celebrates the victory of light over darkness and of good over evil. It is also a time of new beginnings.

People set off fireworks and decorate their homes with small oil lamps.

Everyone eats lots of homemade sweets and gives boxes of sweets as gifts.

Diwali sweets can be made from flour, beans, lentils, carrots, pumpkins, nuts, raisins, and yogurt. Sweet spices such as cinnamon and nutmeg are also used.

Food from a Forest

The Baka are a group of people who live in rainforests in Africa. The Baka are hunter-gatherers. They hunt or find their food in the forest.

Baka men use spears and arrows to hunt for antelopes, crocodiles, and monkeys. Women and children catch fish, turtles, termites, caterpillars, and giant land snails to eat.

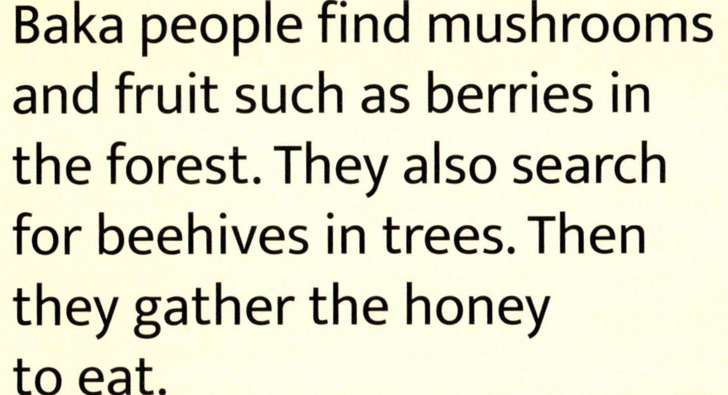

Baka people find mushrooms and fruit such as berries in the forest. They also search for beehives in trees. Then they gather the honey to eat.

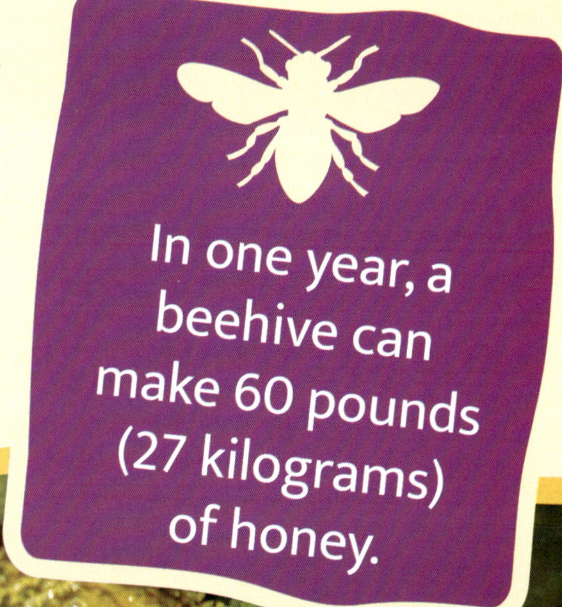

Food from Yaks

Many people around the world get most of the food they eat from their animals. In Tibet, people raise hairy cattle called yaks. Yak farmers get meat and milk from their yaks.

Tibetan people make butter from yak milk. The butter is mixed with water, tea, and salt to make butter tea. This warming, fatty tea is the favorite drink of people in Tibet.

Fish and Chips

In Great Britain, many people love to eat fish and chips. It's traditional to have this food for supper on a Friday night.

Most towns in Great Britain have a fish and chips shop. On Friday nights, there are often long lines of people waiting to buy their food.

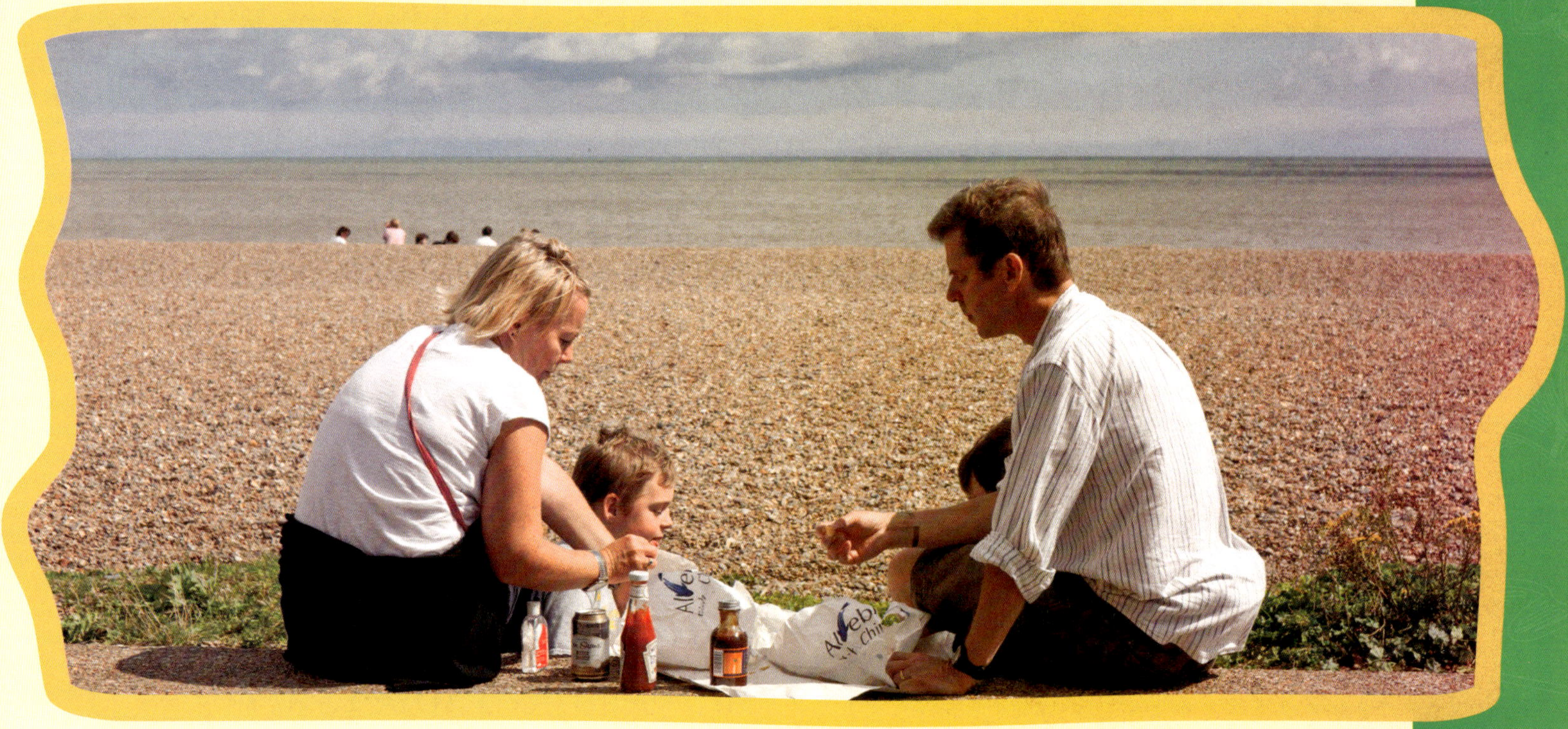

In Great Britain, it's also traditional to eat fish and chips at the seaside, or shore. At the end of a day on the beach, families eat an outdoor supper of fish and chips before heading home.

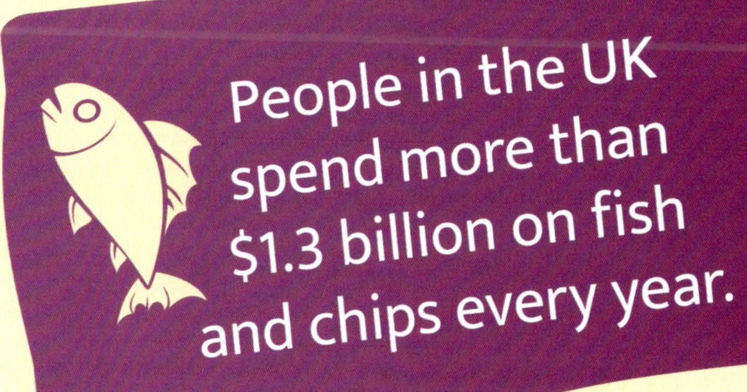

Fasting for Ramadan

For Muslims, Ramadan is the holiest month of the year. During this time, adults and teenagers fast, or don't eat, between sunrise and sunset. Children sometimes fast for just half the day.

Each evening, after sunset, families and friends gather for a special evening meal called *iftar*.

Fasting is a way for Muslims to show their faith in Allah. It also helps people remember that not everyone has enough to eat.

No Food to Eat

Not everyone around the world has enough to eat. Many people are too poor to buy food.

Many people live in places where they cannot grow food. Every night, millions of adults and children go to bed hungry.

In Brazil's cities, many children live on the streets. They have no parents or grown-ups to take care of them. Charities and other helpers try to bring food and drink to the street children.

How is food from around the world the same? How is it different?

What are some of the different ways people get their food?

KEY WORDS

Research has shown that as much as 65 percent of all written material published in English is made up of 300 words. These 300 words cannot be taught using pictures or learned by sounding them out. They must be recognized by sight. This book contains 113 common sight words to help young readers improve their reading fluency and comprehension. This book also teaches young readers several important content words, such as proper nouns. These words are paired with pictures to aid in learning and improve understanding.

Page	Sight Words First Appearance
4	a, and, do, eat, foods, for, in, of, the, we, what
5	all, but, how, is, it, its, like, many, over, people, this, world
6	are, different, grow, important, more, one, plant, than, that, there, very
7	almost, before, from, land, often, places, rivers, some, their, to, use, water, where, with
8	animal, children, day, every, get, just, or, see, your
9	also, faces, into, might, other
10	around, as, by, good, light, new, off, set, small, time
11	be, can, made, such
12	find, group, live, men, they, who
13	make, then, trees
14	most
16	great, have, lines, long, night, on
17	an, at, end, home, year
18	after, between, don't, each, sometimes
19	enough, has, not, show, way
20	go, no, too
21	take, them, try

Page	Content Words First Appearance
4	breakfast, dinner, fries, Germany, Namibia, noodles, porridge, sausage, United States, vegetables
5	black sapote, cheese, chocolate pudding, custard, durian, fruit, Malaysia, Mexico, onions
6	grains, grass, rice, seeds
7	Arkansas, buffaloes, farmers, fields
8	bento boxes, cartoon, character, lunchbox, Japan
9	cars, cubes, eggs, flowers, hot dogs, salmon, seaweed, shapes, superheroes
10	darkness, Diwali, evil, fireworks, Hindu, Jain, lamps, Sikh, sweets
11	beans, carrots, cinnamon, flour, gifts, lentils, nutmeg, nuts, pumpkins, raisins, spices, yogurt
12	Africa, antelopes, arrows, Baka, caterpillars, crocodiles, fish, forest, monkeys, rainforests, snails, spears, termites, turtles, women
13	beehives, berries, honey, mushrooms
14	cattle, meat, milk, Tibet, yaks
15	butter, tea, salt
16	chips, Friday, Great Britain, shop, supper, towns
17	beach, families, seaside, shore
18	adults, fasting, iftar, Muslims, month, Ramadan, sunrise, sunset, teenagers
19	Allah, faith
21	Brazil, charities, drink, helpers, parents, streets

Published by Smartbook Media Inc.
350 5th Avenue, 59th Floor New York, NY 10118
Website: www.openlightbox.com

Copyright © 2019 Smartbook Media Inc.
All rights reserved. No part of this publication may be reproduced, stored in a retrieval system, or transmitted in any form or by any means, electronic, mechanical, photocopying, recording, or otherwise, without the prior written permission of the publisher.

Printed in the United States of America in Brainerd, Minnesota
1 2 3 4 5 6 7 8 9 0 22 21 20 19 18

012018
120117

Library of Congress Cataloging in Publication Control Number: 2017959801

ISBN 978-1-5105-3538-1 (hardcover)
ISBN 978-1-5105-3539-8 (multi-user eBook)

Project Coordinator: John Willis
Art Director: Terry Paulhus

Every reasonable effort has been made to trace ownership and to obtain permission to reprint copyright material. The publisher would be pleased to have any errors or omissions brought to its attention so that they may be corrected in subsequent printings.
The publisher acknowledges Shutterstock and Alamy as its primary image suppliers for this title.